W9-CDZ-412

Mountain Gorillas

by Karen Kane
photographs by Gerry Ellis

Lerner Publications Company • Minneapolis, Minnesota

For all members of the international scientific, conservation, and tourism communities, whose work on mountain gorillas has assured their future. And for Dian Fossey, without whose irascible tenacity the world may not have known just how close it was to losing mountain gorillas forever. —KK

My deepest gratitude to the members of the tracking and anti-poaching patrols, whose dedication over the past decades has received virtually no international recognition, but without whose daily effort in the face of foul weather, harsh living conditions, and civil war we would not have mountain gorillas today. The world owes a tremendous debt to all of you. —GE

Thanks to our series consultant, Sharyn Fenwick, elementary science/math specialist. Mrs. Fenwick was the winner of the National Science Teachers Association 1991 Distinguished Teaching Award. She also was the recipient of the Presidential Award for Excellence in Math and Science Teaching, representing the state of Minnesota at the elementary level in 1992.

Early Bird Nature Books were conceptualized by Ruth Berman and designed by Steve Foley. Series editor is Joelle Riley.

Lerner Publications Company
A division of Lerner Publishing Group
241 First Avenue North
Minneapolis, Minnesota 55401 U.S.A.

Website address: www.lernerbooks.com

Library of Congress Cataloging-in-Publication Data

Kane, Karen.
    Mountain gorillas / Karen Kane ; photographs by Gerry
Ellis.
        p. cm.—(Early bird nature books)
    Includes index.
    ISBN 0-8225-3040-6 (lib. bdg. : alk. paper)
    1. Gorilla—Juvenile literature. 2. Endangered
species—Juvenile literature. I. Ellis, Gerry. II. Title.
III. Series.
QL737.P96 K26 2001
599.884—dc21   00-009366

Manufactured in the United States of America
1 2 3 4 5 6–JR–06 05 04 03 02 01

Contents

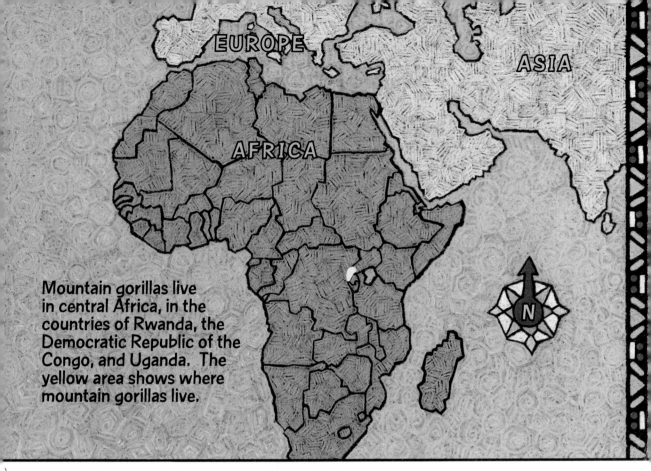

Mountain gorillas live in central Africa, in the countries of Rwanda, the Democratic Republic of the Congo, and Uganda. The yellow area shows where mountain gorillas live.

Be a Word Detective

Can you find these words as you read about the mountain gorilla's life? Be a detective and try to figure out what they mean. You can turn to the glossary on page 46 for help.

blackbacks	**knuckle walking**	**rain forests**
endangered	**nests**	**silverbacks**
extinct	**nurses**	**troop**
habitat	**poachers**	
herbivores	**primates**	

Chapter 1

Gorillas are big and strong. But they are very gentle. What group of animals do gorillas belong to?

Gorillas

Gorillas are gentle, quiet animals. They are much like people. Gorillas can live almost as long as people live. Gorillas play like people. And mother gorillas take care of their babies much like people do.

Gorillas belong to a group of animals called primates (PRYE-mates). Primates have bodies that are shaped like human bodies. And they have hands that are shaped like people's hands. Monkeys, gorillas, and people are all primates.

The word gorilla *means "hairy person."*

A gorilla's big toes work like a person's thumbs. When a gorilla climbs trees, it can hold on to branches with its toes.

Gorillas have arms and legs like people. But gorillas do not walk like people. A gorilla's arms are much longer than ours. Its arms are longer than its legs. A gorilla walks with both its arms and its legs. The gorilla curls its fingers and leans on its knuckles as it walks. This way of walking is called knuckle walking.

Gorillas are big. Male gorillas are bigger than females. A male gorilla is as tall as a grown man. A big male weighs up to 450 pounds. That is as much as seven second graders weigh!

A gorilla can walk like a human for a short distance.
But usually gorillas walk with both their arms and their legs.

A gorilla's body is covered with long fur. The fur is black or dark brown. As a male mountain gorilla gets older, the fur on his back turns silvery-gray. Male gorillas who have silver fur are called silverbacks.

When a male gorilla is about 11 or 12 years old, the hair on his back begins to turn silver. A female gorilla's fur stays black.

This is a lowland gorilla. A lowland gorilla's fur is shorter than a mountain gorilla's fur.

There are two kinds of gorillas in the world. One kind is the mountain gorilla. The other kind is the lowland gorilla. All gorillas live in Africa. And all gorillas live in forests. Mountain gorillas live in forests that are high in the mountains. Lowland gorillas live in forests in lower areas.

Chapter 2

The scientific name of the mountain gorilla is Gorilla gorilla beringei. *What is the weather like where mountain gorillas live?*

Gorillas in the Neighborhood

 Mountain gorillas live in a very tiny area within central Africa. This area is the mountain gorilla's habitat (HAB-uh-tat). A habitat is the area where a kind of animal can live and grow.

Mountain gorillas live high in the mountains.

It rains a lot in the mountain gorilla's habitat. The clouds bump right up against the mountains. The air is foggy, damp, and cool. Mountain gorillas' long fur helps to keep them warm and dry. They have become used to living in such a wet home.

Many rain forests are warm. But the weather is cool in the rain forests where mountain gorillas live.

The mountain gorilla's habitat is covered in rain forests. A rain forest is a thick, wet forest. Most rain forests get more than 80 inches of rain in a year. The mountain gorilla's rain

14

forest has many trees and other plants. Vines and flowers hang from branches. Moss grows on everything. Some plants are covered with thorns or tiny spikes. But that doesn't stop the gorillas. They can easily move through this thick forest.

Plants grow everywhere in the mountain gorilla's habitat.
Mosses and vines grow on other kinds of plants.

This animal is a bushbuck. Bushbucks are small antelopes. They live in the mountain gorilla's habitat.

Mountain gorillas share their habitat with many other animals. Small antelopes move quietly through the forest eating leaves and plants. Big, strong African buffaloes, elephants,

Mountain gorillas share their home with tree hyraxes (top) and Virunga chameleons (bottom).

and pigs also live in the forest. Fuzzy little hyraxes live in tree hollows. Many kinds of birds, frogs, lizards, and colorful insects live in the rain forest, too.

Chapter 3

Gorillas are big. They need to eat lots of food every day. What kinds of food do mountain gorillas eat?

How Was Your Day?

 A mountain gorilla's day is pretty simple. It spends most of its day eating!

Mountain gorillas are herbivores (HUR-buh-vorz). Herbivores are animals who eat only plants. In the rain forest, there are so many plants to eat. Much of the food the gorillas eat grows close to the ground. They eat leaves, tree bark, roots, shoots, flowers, vines, and fruits. Everywhere mountain gorillas go, there is something for them to eat.

Mountain gorillas spend most of their time on the ground. But sometimes they climb trees to get food.

This plant is an African stinging nettle. Mountain gorillas eat the leaves of stinging nettle plants. The gorilla slides the plant through its hand and pulls off a big bunch of leaves at once.

Some of the things mountain gorillas eat may not sound tasty. They eat wild celery. This plant is very, very bitter. Gorillas also eat stinging nettles. Nettles sting people's skin even through clothes!

When mountain gorillas are not eating, they are resting or sleeping. Every night, mountain gorillas make beds to sleep in. The beds are called nests. They are made of vines and branches. Gorillas usually make their nests on the ground. Sometimes gorillas make nests in trees or in holes in tree trunks. A gorilla's nest is shaped like a bowl. It is lined with leafy branches to make it soft. Each gorilla makes its own nest. Do you make your nest every day?

A mountain gorilla's nest is like a cushion made of branches.
The gorilla bends or breaks the branches so they stay flat.

Chapter 4

Mountain gorillas live together in families. What is a family of gorillas called?

Gorilla Families

People have families. Mountain gorillas have families, too. A gorilla family is called a troop. Each troop is made up of 2 to 30 gorillas. The troop travels together, eats together, and sleeps together. Mountain gorillas hardly ever live alone. Living in a troop is safer.

The silverback decides when it is time for his troop to look for food. He also decides when it is time to sleep.

A troop is led by a strong silverback. He is usually the biggest gorilla in the troop. The silverback leads his troop through the forest. He protects his troop from danger. A troop usually has a few male gorillas called blackbacks, too. Blackbacks are younger than silverbacks. A blackback's fur has not yet turned silvery. Several female gorillas, youngsters, and little babies make up the rest of the troop.

Mountain gorillas "talk" to each other. They talk by using sounds and by giving each other special looks. Mountain gorillas roar, purr, belch, grunt, groan, and scream. Each sound means something different.

Gorillas make some kinds of sounds when they are happy. They make different sounds when they are afraid or angry.

These young gorillas are playing. One gorilla is showing its teeth. It is trying to look scary.

Sometimes silverbacks fight. A silverback fights when he is threatened by another silverback. He will also fight when he feels his troop is in danger. A fight is over when one silverback gives in to the other. This usually happens before anyone gets hurt.

When a silverback is angry, he roars very loudly.

When a silverback is protecting his troop from another silverback, he may roar, beat his chest, and wave his arms. He tries to chase the other silverback away. While he is doing this, the other gorillas in his troop can get away.

26

Baby gorillas are especially important to the troop. The adults in the troop will fight to protect young gorillas.

Some animals in the rain forest might try to hurt baby gorillas. But adult gorillas are big and strong. They protect the babies.

Chapter 5

A newborn mountain gorilla has pink skin. The baby's skin turns black in a few days. How much does a newborn gorilla weigh?

Hey Baby!

A mother gorilla gives birth to a baby every four to five years. A baby gorilla weighs 4 to 5 pounds when it is born.

Just like a human baby, a baby gorilla needs its mother for a long time. The baby nurses, or drinks its mother's milk. A baby gorilla nurses until it is three or four years old. During this time, the young gorilla sleeps with its mother in her nest.

A female mountain gorilla is about seven years old when she has her first baby.

A mother gorilla carries her baby through the forest.
The baby gorilla is holding on tightly to its mother's fur.

Baby mountain gorillas can walk when they are about two months old. But their moms carry them most of the time until they are about one year old. A mother gorilla carries her baby on her back or stomach.

A mother gorilla takes good care of her baby. She cuddles the baby and plays with it. She watches over the baby while it learns to live in the forest.

A mother gorilla teaches her baby many things. She shows the baby which plants are good to eat.

Even the silverback is gentle with baby gorillas. He sits still while they climb all over him. He lets them pull his hair. He does not get upset, even if the babies try to wake him up when he is sleeping.

The silverback often plays with the young gorillas.

As a young mountain gorilla gets older, it spends less time with its mother.

When a gorilla is about three years old, it begins to walk with the troop. The troop looks after the young gorilla. If the youngster walks slowly, the troop slows down. If the young gorilla gets tired and stops to rest, the troop waits for it.

When a gorilla is about one year old, it begins to play with other babies. Playing teaches young gorillas how to get along with others.

Young gorillas play for most of the day. They chase one another. They wrestle and tumble. They climb trees and vines. They scramble all over the adult gorillas. They hoot

34

and holler and scream and chuckle. Young gorillas love to play. Often the youngsters want to play when the adults are trying to rest!

Young mountain gorillas play games that look like games human children play. The gorillas play tag, follow the leader, and king of the mountain.

Most young gorillas stay with the troop even after they are grown. But usually when a male gorilla gets old enough to grow silver hair, he leaves the troop. He starts his own family.

This gorilla is almost grown up.

Chapter 6

Once there were more mountain gorillas. Many have died. How many mountain gorillas are left in the world?

A World of Danger

There are only about 600 mountain gorillas in the world. Mountain gorillas are endangered. That means that if people don't work hard to save mountain gorillas, they may all die. Then mountain gorillas would be extinct. When a kind of animal is extinct, it is gone forever.

There are many reasons why mountain gorillas are endangered. One reason is that some of their habitat has been made into farmland. People need farmland to grow food and other crops. Sometimes people cut down trees in the mountain gorilla's habitat. Then they grow crops on the land.

There are farms right next to the rain forests where mountain gorillas live.

These men have found an antelope trap. Sometimes gorillas get their hands or feet caught in antelope traps.

People used to hunt mountain gorillas, but they don't anymore. It is against the law to hunt mountain gorillas. It is also against the law to hunt the other animals in the gorillas' habitat. But some people hunt the other animals anyway. These people are called poachers. Poachers set traps for antelopes. Sometimes gorillas get hurt by these traps.

Living in a troop helps mountain gorillas. The gorillas take care of the other members of their troop.

Another danger to mountain gorillas is war. The people in the countries where the gorillas live sometimes fight. Soldiers move through the forest. They scare the gorillas. Sometimes frightened gorillas get lost. They can't find the other members of their troop. It is dangerous for a gorilla to be alone in the forest.

40

The mountain gorilla's habitat is protected. It is in a national park. The national park has guards who protect the gorillas. Every day, guards go into the forest. The guards check on the gorillas to make sure they are safe. The guards take traps away and arrest poachers.

In the national park, people work hard to keep the mountain gorillas safe.

Scientists come to the rain forest to learn more about mountain gorillas.

There are no mountain gorillas in zoos. The only way people can see mountain gorillas is to visit their habitat in Africa. When people visit the gorillas, they help to save them. Visitors to the park pay money to visit the gorillas. The money is used to help protect the gorillas.

Mountain gorillas are beautiful, gentle creatures. They have lived on the earth for many years. People are working hard to save them. It is up to us to make sure mountain gorillas will have a safe place to live forever.

If people take care of the mountain gorilla's habitat, the gorillas and many other kinds of animals will have a good place to live.

On Sharing a Book

As you know, adults greatly influence a child's attitude toward reading. When a child sees you read, or when you share a book with a child, you're sending a message that reading is important. Show the child that reading a book together is important to you. Find a comfortable, quiet place. Turn off the television and limit other distractions, such as telephone calls.

Be prepared to start slowly. Take turns reading parts of this book. Stop and talk about what you're reading. Talk about the photographs. You may find that much of the shared time is spent discussing just a few pages. This discussion time is valuable for both of you, so don't move through the book too quickly. If the child begins to lose interest, stop reading. Continue sharing the book at another time. When you do pick up the book again, be sure to revisit the parts you have already read. Most importantly, enjoy the book!

Be a Vocabulary Detective

You will find a word list on page 5. Words selected for this list are important to the understanding of the topic of this book. Encourage the child to be a word detective and search for the words as you read the book together. Talk about what the words mean and how they are used in the sentence. Do any of these words have more than one meaning? You will find these words defined in a glossary on page 46.

What about Questions?

Use questions to make sure the child understands the information in this book. Here are some suggestions:

> What did this paragraph tell us? What does this picture show? What do you think we'll learn about next? How are gorillas like humans? How are they different? How does a gorilla walk? Where do mountain gorillas live? What do they eat? Where does a mountain gorilla sleep? How does a young mountain gorilla play? What are some dangers to mountain gorillas? What do you think it is like being a mountain gorilla? What is your favorite part of the book? Why?

If the child has questions, don't hesitate to respond with questions of your own such as: What do *you* think? Why? What is it that you don't know? If the child can't remember certain facts, turn to the index.

Introducing the Index

The index is an important learning tool. It helps readers get information quickly without searching throughout the whole book. Turn to the index on page 47. Choose an entry, such as *eating,* and ask the child to use the index to find out what foods mountain gorillas eat. Repeat this exercise with as many entries as you like. Ask the child to point out the differences between an index and a glossary. (The index helps readers find information quickly, while the glossary tells readers what words mean.)

Where in the World?

Many plants and animals found in the Early Bird Nature Books series live in parts of the world other than the United States. Encourage the child to find the places mentioned in this book on a world map or globe. Take time to talk about climate, terrain, and how you might live in such places.

All the World in Metric!

Although our monetary system is in metric units (based on multiples of 10), the United States is one of the few countries in the world that does not use the metric system of measurement. Here are some conversion activities you and the child can do using a calculator:

WHEN YOU KNOW:	MULTIPLY BY:	TO FIND:
miles	1.609	kilometers
feet	0.3048	meters
inches	2.54	centimeters
gallons	3.787	liters
tons	0.907	metric tons
pounds	0.454	kilograms

Activities

Visit a zoo to see gorillas. How are the gorillas in the zoo similar to other primates, such as monkeys? How are they different?

Mountain gorillas use many special looks and gestures to "talk" to one another. See if you can talk like a gorilla. Set aside 30 minutes during which you and your family or friends will use no words. You may grunt, touch objects or people, and use gestures or facial expressions, but you may not use any written or spoken words. Can you get your ideas across to other people? Can you understand what your friends or family are saying to you?

Glossary

blackbacks: young male gorillas whose fur has not begun to turn silver

endangered: only a few of a kind of animal are still living

extinct: no members of a kind of animal are still living

habitat (HAB-uh-tat): the area where a kind of animal can live and grow

herbivores (HUR-buh-vorz): animals who eat only plants

knuckle walking: leaning on the knuckles while walking

nests: beds that mountain gorillas make out of vines and branches

nurses: drinks mother's milk

poachers: people who hunt animals even though it is against the law

primates (PRYE-mates): animals who have bodies shaped like human bodies. Monkeys, gorillas, and people are all primates.

rain forests: very thick forests where a lot of rain falls

silverbacks: older male gorillas who have silver fur on their back

troop: a family of gorillas

Index

Pages listed in **bold** type refer to photographs.

About the Author

Author, naturalist, and conservationist Karen Kane is an active participant in promoting the understanding and appreciation of Earth's wilds. Widely traveled, she has studied wildlife and the environment for much of her life. Her interest in wildlife—particularly gorillas—has been heightened by observing wild animals in their natural habitats. This is the third book she has produced with her husband, photographer Gerry Ellis. Karen and Gerry make their home in Portland, Oregon.

About the Photographer

Gerry Ellis communicates his passion for the natural world through his award-winning wildlife and nature photography. A dedicated naturalist, he has explored the world for nearly two decades, visiting every continent in his quest to experience nature in its wildest and purest forms. His interest in great apes has taken him to remote areas of Africa, where he has worked with both mountain and lowland gorillas as well as chimpanzees, and to Borneo, where he has tracked wild orangutans. Gerry's images of wildlife and nature have been awarded top honors, including several in the BBC Wildlife Photographer of the Year competition. Among his many publications are the Lerner Publishing Group titles *African Elephants*, *Cheetahs*, *Hippos*, *Rhinos*, *Slugs*, and *Zebras*. He lives with his wife, Karen, in Portland, Oregon.

The Early Bird Nature Books Series

African Elephants
Alligators
Ants
Apple Trees
Bobcats
Brown Bears
Cats
Cougars
Crayfish
Dandelions
Dolphins
Giant Sequoia Trees
Herons
Jellyfish

Manatees
Moose
Mountain Goats
Mountain Gorillas
Ostriches
Peacocks
Penguins
Polar Bears
Popcorn Plants
Prairie Dogs
Rats
Red-Eyed Tree Frogs
Saguaro Cactus
Sandhill Cranes

Scorpions
Sea Lions
Sea Turtles
Slugs
Swans
Tarantulas
Tigers
Venus Flytraps
Vultures
Walruses
Whales
Wild Turkeys
Zebras